INUIT
OF THE
NORTH

Allan C. Bennett
William E. Flannigan
Marilyn P. Hladun

Fitzhenry & Whiteside

INUIT OF THE NORTH

Canadian Cataloguing in Publication Data

Bennett, Allan C.
 Inuit of the North

(Inside Communities/First Nations series)
First published 1972 under title: Eskimo: Journey
Through Time, 1981 Inuit Community

For use in schools
ISBN 0-88902-052-3

I. Inuit - Canada.* I. Flannigan, William E.
II. Hladun, Marilyn P. III. Title. IV. Title:
Eskimo: journey through time. V. Series:
Inside communities series
E99.E7B46 1980   970.004'97   C94-0094427-5

Acknowledgements

Consulting Editor	James Forrester
Authors	Allan Bennett
	William Flannigan
	Marilyn Hladun
Editors	Ian Gillen
	Jane Lind
	Nick Stephens
Design	Arne Roosman

Printed and bound in Canada

Contents

Photographs

Austin Airways, 5
Fred Breummer, 3, 14, 16, 41, 64
Fédération des Coopératives
du Nouveau-Québec, 8, 63
Gouvernement du Québec, 60-61
Miller Services, 35, 55
John Smith, 15, 54, 56
Toronto Star Limited, 27
Toronto-Dominion Bank, 6, 11, 14, 16, 22, 23, 57
West Baffin Cooperative Ltd., 23
Winnipeg Art Gallery/Ernest Mayer, 21

Maps

Acorn Technical Art

Illustrations

Vlasta Van Kampen
Arne Roosman (cover)

SALLUIT, AN INUIT COMMUNITY

Hello, my name is Naullaq. I am an Inuk. My family and I are Inuit. Some people call us Eskimos, but we don't like that word. The name we use for ourselves is Inuit, which means "the people." My family and I live in Salluit, at the very northern tip of Quebec. You would probably spell it Sugluk, but we prefer Salluit. I would like to show you my community. You can come and visit me in Salluit. We can hunt and play together. We can talk about how the Inuit live and about how we used to live in the old days.

Did You Know?

Inuk means "man" or "person" in Inuktitut. Inuit is the plural of Inuk. Inuktitut is the name for the language spoken by the Inuit.

The word "Eskimo" comes from the Indian phrase *wigas-ki-mowak* which means eaters of raw meat.

When Inuktitut is written down, the words are sometimes spelt in several different ways.
The name of Naullaq's village is a good example:

Sugluk is the spelling that has been commonly used in English in the past.

Saglouc is the French spelling, and until recently this was the official version that was used on maps, since the village is located in Quebec.

Salluit is the spelling that the Inuit themselves prefer, and in 1980 it was agreed this would become the official name in future.

3

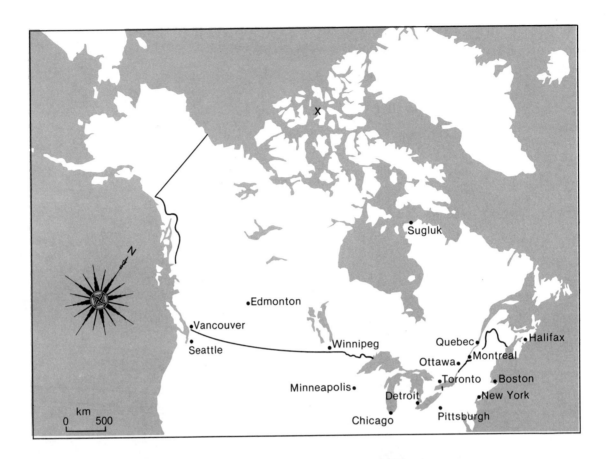

1. Find Salluit on the map. Where is it in relation to your community? About how far is your home from Salluit?

2. If you wanted to visit Salluit how would you get there? What different routes and means of transport might you use?

3. What problems and difficulties might you face in travelling to Salluit?

4. How do you think people get from place to place within Salluit?

5. What problems would the people face in building roads and highways in Salluit?

6. Other than flying, how do you think people travel between Salluit and other communities?

Things To Do

Trace or sketch the map above, then:
1. Look in an atlas or geography book and find the tree line. Mark it on your map. What does this suggest about Salluit?

2. On your map, find and label Siberia, Alaska, Baffin Island, Greenland, Labrador, Arctic Ocean, Atlantic Ocean, Hudson Bay, James Bay, Ungava Bay, Frobisher Bay, Hudson Strait.

3. Can you find out what is located at the point marked X on the map? Why is this an important thing to know about?

4. Find the Arctic Circle and mark it on your map. What does it signify? Why is it important?

NORD-OUEST et les ILES BAFFINS.

Flt/Vol 211 Tuesday/Mardi		Flt/Vol 213 Saturday/Samedi		Flt/Vol 207 Mon. to Fri./ Lundi au vendredi			Flt/Vol 208 Mon. to Fri./ Lundi au vendredi	
Arr.	Dep.	Arr.	Dep.	Arr.	Dep.		Arr.	Dep.
					0800	TIMMINS	1635	
(Overnight stop required at Great Whale or Povungnituk from points south to Sugluk, Ivugivik, Akulivik and Cape Dorset.)				0820 ·	0825	· COCHRANE ·	1610 ·	1615
				0910	0940	MOOSONEE	1450	1515
(Arrèt de nuit requis a Great Whale ou Po-vungnituk en Provenance sud de Sugluk, Ivugivik, Akulivik et Cap Dorset.)				1015	1025	·· RUPERT HOUSE ··	1405	1415
				1050	1100	EASTMAIN	1330	1340
				1125	1135	PAINT HILLS	1255	1305
				1200	1220	FORT GEORGE	1210	1230
	0800		0800	1310	1340	GREAT WHALE	1050	1120
				1420	1430	SANIKILUAQ	1000	1010
0930	0945	0930	0945	1530	1540	PORT HARRISON	0850	0900
1035	1050	1035	1050	1630	1645	POVUNGNITUK	1750	0800
1120	1130			1715		··· AKULIVIK ···		1720
1215	1230					IVUGIVIK		
1305		1200	1210			**Salluit**		
		1305				CAPE DORSET		

· Stops at Cochrane Monday, Wednesday & Friday Only / Arrèts a Cochrane lundi, mercredi et vendredi.
·· Aircraft change at Moosonee / Changement d'avion a Moosonee
··· *Tuesday & Friday only / Mardi et Vendredi seulement.

Akulivik (Cape Smith)

129.	Belcher Islands (Sanikiluaq)												
116.	210	Cape Dorset											
			Eastmain										
				Fort Chimo									
			42.		Fort George								
160.	36.	243.	83.	154.	42.	Great Whale (Poste-de-la-Baleine)							
45.	166.	91.			229.	198.	Ivugivik						
250.	149.	317.	53.	263.	78.	112.	278.	Moosonee					
			25.		25.	64.		63.	Paint Hills				
79.	49.	160.			181.	128.	85.	112.	181.	151.	Port Harrison (Inoucdjouac)		
33.	101.	109.			131.	173.	131.	62.	224.	196.	49.	Povungnituk	
			25.			63.	100.		30.	42.			Rupert House
59.	159.	59.				189.	30.	278.		107.	59.		**Salluit**
292.	184.	352.	95.	298.	112.	149.	317.	56.	104.	224.	263.	79.	317.	Timmins

PASSENGER FARES
PRIX DU VOYAGEUR

(One way/billet simple)

Note
To calculate fares that are not shown
add the prices of sectors shown.

"A Flight Schedule for the North"

The airplane is a lifeline for Salluit.

1. What does this statement mean? Do you think it is true? Would the airplane be Salluit s only lifeline? What other lifeline(s) might Salluit have?

2. What lifeline did the people of Salluit have before airplanes were invented?

3. Using an atlas, locate the towns on the flight schedule and mark them on your map. Trace the flight from Timmins to Salluit (Sugluk).

4. According to the schedule, how long would it take to get to Salluit from Timmins? Why is it not a direct flight? How might weather affect the schedule?

5

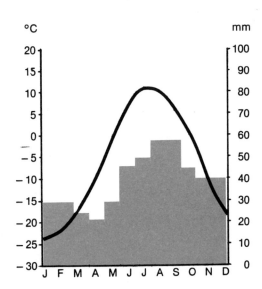

1. According to the climograph, what is the average temperature during the winter at Salluit? What is the temperature like during the summer?

2. How many months have temperatures
   (a) above freezing and
   (b) below freezing?

3. During what months is precipitation heaviest? When is it least?

4. What kind of precipitation would Salluit have during the months with freezing temperatures?

5. How do you think the Arctic climate would affect the activities of the Inuit?

6. Try to find out what the climate figures are for your community and compare them with the figures from Salluit.

Something To Think About

1. How many centimetres of snowfall equal one centimetre of rainfall?

2. Estimate how much snow would fall at Salluit during the months with freezing temperatures.

3. How much snow falls in your community during an average winter?

4. Most people think of the Arctic as "a land of ice and snow." How does your answer to question 2 relate to this?

1. Use a thermometer to help you construct a graph of the temperature at four-hour intervals throughout one full day.
    The newspaper or radio station might give you the temperature during the night.
    If a minimum and maximum thermometer is available in your science room, it could be used. Calculate the *minimum*, the *maximum* and the range for the day. Compare the results with the graph from Salluit.

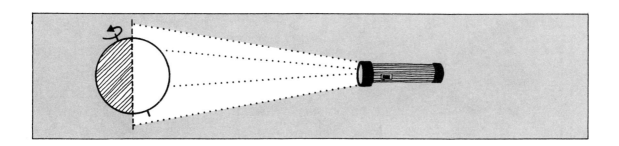

2. Mark the approximate location of Salluit and your town on a globe with chalk.
    Turn the lights off and shine a flashlight or light from a projector directly over the equator to represent the sun. Tilt the globe slightly *away* from the light. Now rotate the globe. You have recreated the day and night cycle of the earth when it is winter in the Northern Hemisphere. The area in shadow represents that part of the world where it is nighttime and dark. What do you notice about the pole areas as you rotate the globe?

3. Repeat the experiment with the globe tilted *towards* the light. Now you are recreating the day and night cycle of the earth when it is summer in the Northern Hemisphere.

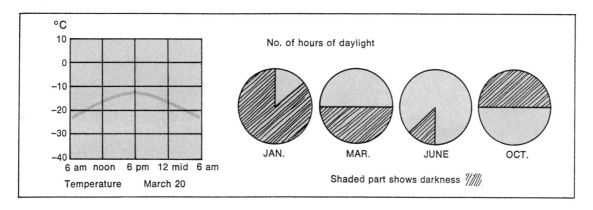

4. Look at the diagram above.
    What was the lowest temperature for the day?
    What was the highest? What was the temperature range for the day?

5. Look at the diagrams to the right.
    How is the graph related to the diagram for March? Would it be the same for October? Why or why not?

6. What would the graph probably be like for January? For June?
    Explain your answer.

Kanguq   Nuna   Iqaluk   Paani   Grandma   Naullaq   Tuttu   Grandpa

Naullaq's house

There are eight people in my family: Kanguq, my father, and Igaluq, my Mother; my brothers Tuttu, who is nine, and Nuna, who is five. You've already met Paani, my sister, who is seven. I'm the oldest—I'm twelve. And there are Grandma and Grandpa who live with us too. We live in a wooden house that was built by the government. Grandma and Grandpa miss the old-style homes they lived in before they moved to Salluit. In the old days the people lived in tents during the summer and moved from place to place in search of caribou to hunt. In winter they would build snowhouses and hunt seals through the sea ice. Now we stay in one place all year round, but I still like to hear the stories Grandma and Grandpa tell about the old days.

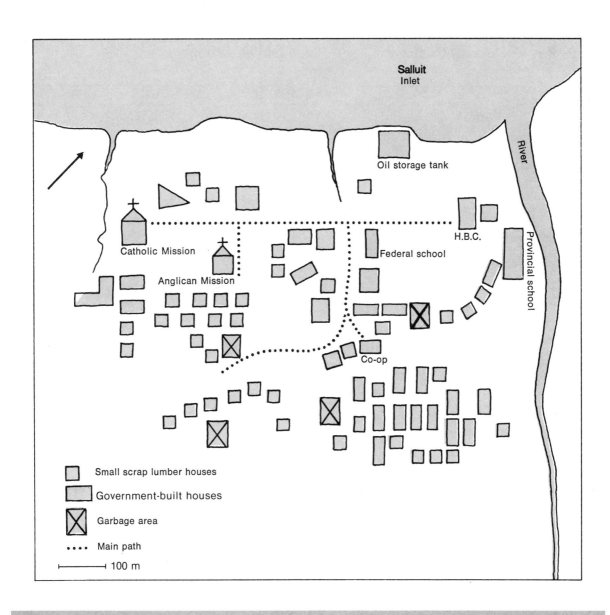

Salluit
Inlet

River

Oil storage tank

Catholic Mission

Anglican Mission

H.B.C.

Federal school

Provincial school

Co-op

☐ Small scrap lumber houses

☐ Government-built houses

☒ Garbage area

•••• Main path

├────┤ 100 m

Salluit Community Plan

1. Look carefully at the community plan and the photograph of the town.

2. Compare the symbols on the plan with the buildings in the picture.

3. How many families do you think live in Salluit?

4. Why would there be two churches in such a small settlement?

5. What public services are found in Salluit?

Hudson's Bay Co. Manager's House

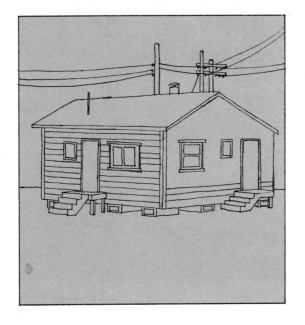

Naullaq's Home

Manager's home has 3 bedrooms and a bath

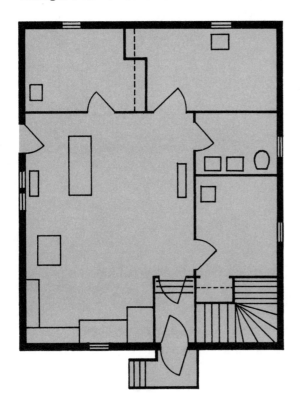

One-bedroom government-supplied home

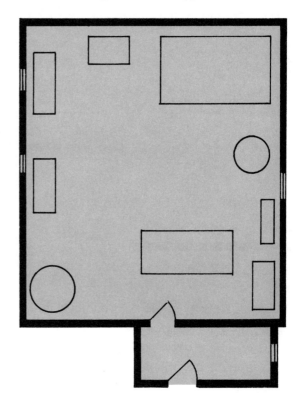

1. Compare the floor plan and furnishings of Naullaq's home, the Hudson's Bay Company Manager's home and your own home.

2. What materials are used to build the homes?

3. How is your house protected from freezing temperatures during the winter?

4. How would the location of Salluit affect (a) the kind of building materials used and (b) the cost of building?

Water is delivered to Salluit homes every two days by a large water truck called a Muskeg. The water is supplied by the government for a small charge.

The bases of the hydro poles in Salluit are painted with fluorescent stripes to help reduce Skidoo accidents.

Salluit houses first became permanent homes in the early 1970s when the government decided Inuit children should attend school.

1. Why do you think water is delivered by truck in Salluit? What problems would there be in using piped water, as is usual further south? Can you suggest a way of solving this problem in northern communities like Salluit?

Special problems

People who live in northern areas face special problems. For example:

1. They have to be extra careful handling liquids like gasoline and kerosene, because if such liquids come into contact with bare skin in cold weather they can cause instant frost bite.

2. Further south it is a good idea not to let moist bare skin touch metal outside in winter. In the north, people must avoid doing so at all costs.

3. Special care has to be taken of hands, feet and face during winter. Boots and socks must be heavy enough for warmth but loose enough to allow proper circulation.
If your feet hurt, you are okay.
If they hurt and then stop hurting, you have to investigate immediately.

Think about the special conditions that exist in the North. What other problems might they cause for people living there?

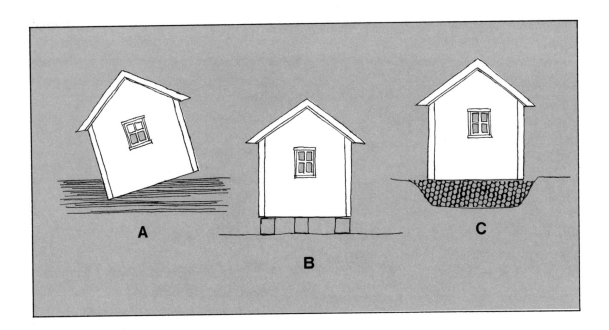

The Permafrost Puzzle

1. In diagram A, what problem occurs when the heat from the house melts the top layer of the frozen soil?

2. In diagrams B and C, what changes have been made to prevent this from happening?

3. How does the use of gravel help to prevent melting of the permafrost?

Find out about the special costs and problems involved in building houses in the north.

Did You Know?

In the Arctic region, most of the ground is frozen all year round. This is called permafrost. Only the top metre or two of ground have a chance to thaw in summer. Permafrost underlies as much as one-fifth of all the land areas in the world. In Canada, it underlies between 40% and 50% of the land.

No one really knows when the permafrost started. Along the southern part of the Arctic coast it may reach down for as little as three or four metres, but in the high Arctic islands it is known to penetrate as much as five hundred metres below the surface. Geophysicists think it probably began in the cold periods of the Pleistocene Age.

Today in both Canada and Russia, permafrost is forming in some areas, retreating in others. It does not lie beneath the lakes, but when an island forms or a sandbar builds up in a river, permafrost begins to form in the soil immediately. Permafrost has good and bad sides. It discourages plant growth, yet if it was not there to support the thawed soil and water above it in summer, there would be no vegetation at all over large stretches of the Arctic.

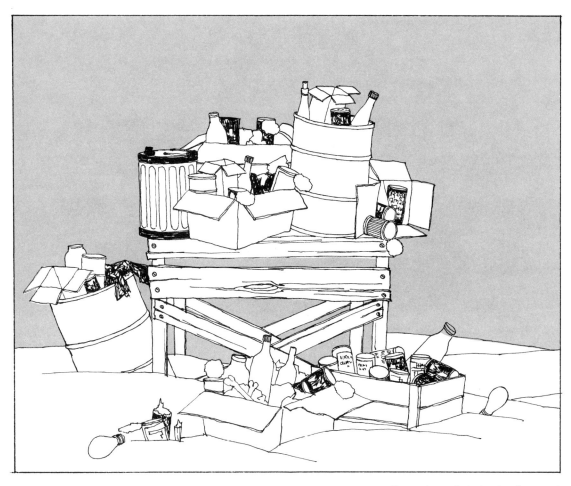

Sewage and garbage disposal

Sewage and garbage is placed on a community platform. When there is no more space left on the platform, the refuse is taken out of the village and left on the ice, or it is thrown in the river.

1. What problems would the sewage and garbage create during the warm months of the year? Why do the same problems not exist during the winter?

2. Why does Salluit not install a regular sewage system?

3. Compare sewage and garbage disposal in Salluit to sewage and garbage disposal in your community.

Traditional umiaks have been replaced by power-driven Peterhead fishing boats.

Goods from the annual supply ship are carried to the settlement's warehouses.

SHOPPING IN SALLUIT

The Hudson's Bay Company Store

The Salluit Co-op

1. In what stores does your family shop for clothes, food, furniture, appliances?

2. What other stores might you visit?

3. Where are most of these stores found in your community?

4. Of what value is a central business district to a shopper? What other kinds of shopping districts are there?

5. Where is the central business district of Salluit? Why are transportation routes important in this area?

6. What other buildings are included in Salluit's business district?

Things To Do

Make a survey of the shops in your community? Where are they located? Are they grouped together, as in Salluit, or are they spread out?

The Salluit Co-op

The Salluit Co-op was started during the middle 1960s. The early years were difficult and uncertain. The Co-op experimented with several different ways of making money, such as buying and selling the food and furs that were brought in by the hunters. In 1967 the Fédération des Coopératives du Nouveau-Québec was formed. With the help of the Fédération, the Salluit Co-op was reorganized and expanded. The Quebec government donated a large building which contains the Co-op's store, warehouse and office. One of the main purposes of the Co-op is to give the people a place to sell their carvings. The Co-op has become the centre of soapstone carving, sale and distribution. The artists can take cash for their work, or they can use it as credit for buying food, clothing or other goods.

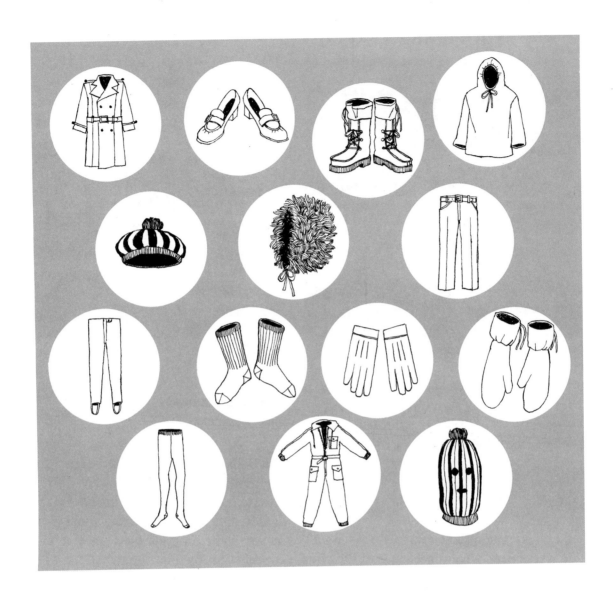

Clothing: Traditional vs. Modern

What types of clothing would you take with you to the Arctic regions on a trip? Why? What kinds of materials give the greatest warmth?

Did You Know?

Life is expensive in Salluit because most of the things the Inuit need must be brought in from the outside. Freight costs are high, and increase the prices of things. The cheapest way of bringing in goods is by sea during the summer. This also provides jobs for the people loading and unloading the supply boats.

Paani, in old style parka and sealskin boots.

Her friends wear modern windproof snowsuits.

Things To Do

Try to collect as many different types of materials as you can.

On a chart, list these materials.

Cover your hands with samples of the materials. Pick up a few ice cubes. Hold them in your hands a few minutes.

Record on your chart which materials best protect your hands from the cold (ratings: warm, cool, cold).

What change has taken place in the clothing worn by the Inuit as a result of the establishment of trading posts and stores?

In the old days, the women made all the clothing for their family from the skins of the animals killed by the hunters. Nowadays the people use factory-made clothing bought from the Hudson's Bay store, or purchased C.O.D. from mail-order companies.

1950 Shopping List

1990 Shopping List

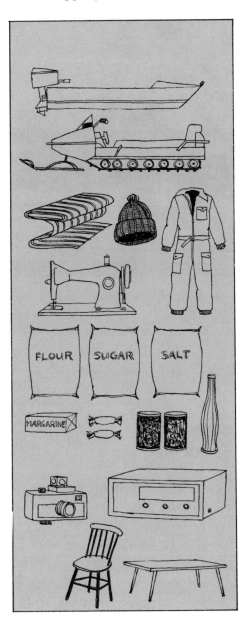

Transportation

Clothes

Food

Miscellaneous

1. Compare the two shopping lists.
   How have they changed in forty years?

2. What has caused this change? How might
   this change put new burdens on the Inuit?

	Cost	Wearing Ability	Availability
1900			
1990			

Discuss the column showing the availability of materials in 1900. Do research to complete the remaining columns of the chart.

Where Does the Money Come From?

1. Make a list of the ways you can earn money to buy things.

2. What ways do the Inuit have of earning money?

3. In your dictionary, find the meaning of the word co-operative.

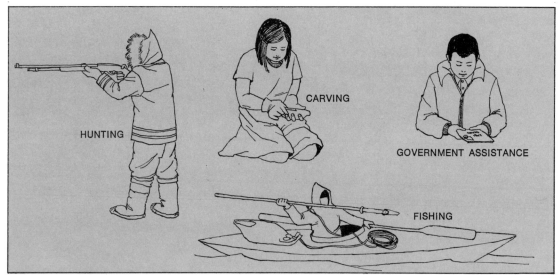

HUNTING

CARVING

GOVERNMENT ASSISTANCE

FISHING

4. Who would be in charge of the Co-op and the handling of the money?

5. Who decides on the value of the items.

6. Where will the Co-op sell the goods it buys from the people?

7. How can the profits made by the Co-op be used to help the Inuit?

8. To what extent are the Inuit dependent on
   a) government?
   b) co-operatives?
   c) each other?

9. If everyone in the village belongs to the Co-op, why would people still shop in the Bay? Think of
   a) the past.
   b) how big and rich the Hudson's Bay Company is.

Things To Do

1. Set up a co-op in the classroom.
   Bring in items from home to trade or sell.
   Decide among yourselves how to manage the co-op and how to buy and sell. How can the classroom use the profits?

2. What can you find out about other kinds of co-ops?
   a) farmers' co-ops
   b) food co-ops
   c) apartment co-ops
   d) others.

For centuries the Inuit have been fine artists and craftsmen. Carving was one type of art that was practised by many Inuit, especially the hunters. Amulets were a common type of carving. An amulet is a small carving showing an animal, a person, or a spirit. In the old days, the Inuit wore amulets in the belief that they would bring good luck in the hunt, or ward off evil spirits.

Another kind of art was practised by the women. As they made the clothes for the family, they liked to decorate them with bold patterns and interesting figures. The women became skilled at cutting these shapes out of seal and caribou skin and sewing them onto the clothing to make striking decorations.

Through their art, the Inuit made beautiful things for use in their daily lives. They also used their art to express their feelings for the land and the animals and plants around them, as well as the spirits that they believed live in all things. Inuit art is now an important source of income for the people of the North. As well, it is serving as a way for the Inuit to preserve a record of the old ways, before these are lost.

Woman Holding Child, by Mary Saviadyuk

James Houston

In 1948, a young artist named James Houston came to Port Harrison (Inoucdjouac) on Hudson Bay to make drawings of the Inuit and their way of life. As an artist, Houston was excited by the carvings he saw, and he recognized immediately the skill of the Inuit artists. Perhaps, he wondered, people in the south would also appreciate the carvings and would buy them to put in their homes. Over the next two years he returned many times to the north, visiting many Inuit settlements including Salluit, buying carvings for sale in the south. The carvings were an instant hit and nowadays many people across Canada and around the world receive pleasure from carvings made by the skilled hands of Inuit artists. Since those early days, Inuit in many communities have tried other art forms with success. Inuit artists are now known for their beautiful prints, tapestries and drawings in addition to their carvings.

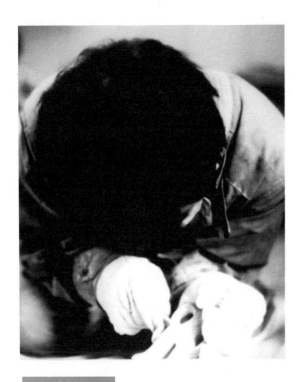

Things To Do

Visit your library to learn what kind of rock soapstone is and where it is found.

Did You Know?

1. Raw stone for carvings is becoming increasingly hard to obtain and often involves long trips.

2. The cost of the stone itself makes up about half of the final price of a carving.

3. As well as useful objects like oarlocks and snowknives, beautiful miniature carvings were made from walrus ivory. The tiny carvings originated as charms to bring luck on the hunt. Walrus tusks incised with pictures became record sticks of important events.

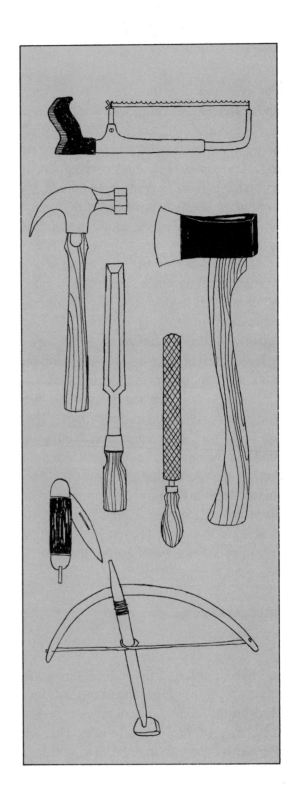

What are these tools used for?

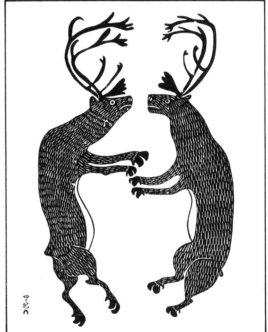

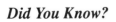

Did You Know?

The symbols at the base of the print represent the names of

a) the artist
b) the sculptor
c) the Co-op

The Canadian government has created an "Igloo Tag" to identify authentic Inuit carving. Unfortunately, replica manufacturers try to copy Inuit art to sell to people looking for inexpensive souvenirs. A person can be sure a sculpture is genuine when this tag appears on a work.

In 1970, the Canadian government passed a law declaring soapstone a "non-mineral" in the Northwest Territories. This was done to protect the Inuit from companies with mining rights. These companies might otherwise cut off the free supply of soapstone the Inuit need for their carvings. In Quebec, soapstone is specially mentioned in the Northern Quebec Agreement that was signed with the Inuit in 1975. The agreement guarantees that soapstone in Category 1 lands belongs to the local community and the people can mine it without charge.

Before 1959, Salluit carvings were big and primitive and were not as popular as more appealing carvings from other areas. Then this primitive style abruptly disappeared and in 1961 new carvings began to appear. There was a shift from light to dark stone, from rough surfaces to smooth.

This shift seems to represent an overall trend in Inuit sculpture. It is becoming increasingly less primitive and more classic. This may be due to the harder stone now being used, with its finer grain. Or it may be that the new kind of sculpture sells more widely.

Whatever the reason, some critics regret the disappearance of the earlier, more massive style.

Things To Do

Make your own prints for special occasions. You could use potatoes, sponges, linoleum blocks, wood blocks, printers' ink, etc.

Make your own carvings. You could use soap, wood, maple rock, soapstone, plaster of Paris (vermiculite), etc.

THE HUNT

A Caribou Hunt

There is great excitement in the village today. A herd of caribou has been seen approaching Payne Lake. It is a big herd, and it has been a long time since there were enough caribou to cause much interest in Salluit. Naullaq's father and grandfather and several of their friends have decided to go on a caribou hunt.

Naullaq is especially excited. "Can't I go with you?" he asks. "Please, can I, Dad? I'm old enough to be a hunter."

"Yes," replies his father with a smile. "You can come with us, as long as you promise that you'll work hard in school to make up for the time you'll lose while we're away. It's important to know how to be a good hunter, but it's also important to keep up with your work at the school."

Things To Do

Pretend you are Naullaq. Write a diary telling about the hunting trip day by day.

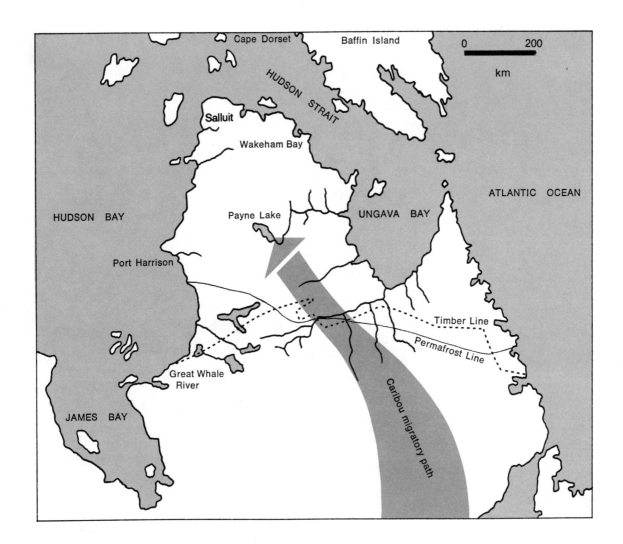

1. What relationships can be noticed on the map between the Timber Line and the Permafrost Line?

2. What is the meaning of each line?

3. If you flew over this region in an airplane, would you be able to see these lines on the landscape? Why?

4. How would each of these regions that are separated by a line affect
   a) the animals of the region?
   b) the people of the region?

5. The trip to Payne Lake will take the hunters three days. How far will they travel each day? Refer to the scale.

Naullaq's father and the other hunters load up their snowmobiles the night before in order to get an early start the next morning.

1. Pretend that you are going on the caribou hunt. Make a list of supplies and equipment you would take with you.

2. Compare your list with those of others in the class. What differences are there? What similarities?

3. What do the words *speed, distance, weight* and *efficiency* make you think of in relation to the hunt? How do these thoughts affect your choice of equipment?

Something To Think About

Pretend it is 500 years ago. There is no such thing as a snowmobile, a rifle, or metal tools. There is no store to buy food or clothing in.

You are going on a caribou hunt. Make a list of supplies and equipment you would take with you. How do considerations of speed, distance, weight, and efficiency affect your list?

The Hunt Begins

Some of the young men have not been on a caribou hunt before. They ask Grandfather for his advice on the best ways to hunt the caribou. Grandfather has been on many hunts in his life and knows all the tricks.

"I will tell you some things about tuktuk," says Grandfather. "If you think about these things, you should be able to work out a technique for hunting him. First of all, tuktuk can run very fast for short distances, fast enough to outrun a wolf or dog. Tuktuk has poor eyesight, but a keen sense of smell. Finally, tuktuk is a very cautious animal, but he is also curious and likes to investigate anything that appears unusual."

1. Using Grandfather's information, work out a plan for hunting the caribou. Discuss your ideas with others in the class. Whose plan made the best use of all the information?

2. What would be the advantages and disadvantages of using a tent or a snowhouse for shelter on the trail?

Did You Know?

The Inuit sometimes use traditional ways of life when they are on the trail and away from the village, such as building a small snowhouse for overnight shelter.

A typical dinner menu for the hunters might be: bannock, frozen fish and tea. Bannock is a good bread to take on a hunting trip. The mixture of flour, baking powder and fat is pressed flat in the bottom of a pan and each side is cooked for 10 minutes over a lamp. It can be stored for long periods of time.

Today, instead of using their traditional kooliks (soapstone lamps), many Inuit use portable camp stoves for cooking. Sometimes they use oil drums cut in half in which they burn wood scraps or brush.

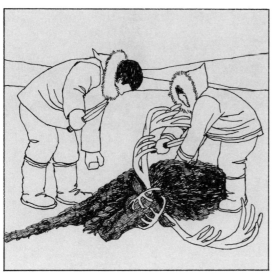

1. According to the illustrations, what is done to the caribou after it is killed?

2. Some of the meat is being *cached*. What does this mean? Why is it done?

3. Will the meat go bad? Why or why not? What other way might the meat be lost? How will the hunters try to avoid this?

1. Naullaq's caribou hunt takes place at the end of March. How many hours of daylight do the hunters have?

2. What hardships might the hunters face on their journey? What dangers might there be?

3. Snowmobiles, unlike dogs, cannot smell their way home. How might the hunters find their way home in bad weather?

4. Look carefully at the sketch to find a disadvantage to Skidoo travel.

5. What happened to the two machines?

6. What feature of the Arctic landscape was responsible for the damage?

7. If you were on a trip like this, what would you bring to help avoid being stranded by a damaged machine?

8. What advantages would a dog team have over a Skidoo for a trip?

This is the plane the men chartered to bring back the caribou and the broken snowmobiles.

1. How has the plane been adapted for use in the Arctic?

2. How could the plane be changed for landing during different seasons of the year?

3. Do you think an airplane is the usual method of bringing home caribou from a hunt? What other method might be used?

If you lived in the Arctic with few tools or weapons, how would you use the parts of the Caribou hide, antlers, sinews, muscle) for the articles shown below?

Hide, Antlers, Sinews, Muscle.

GROUND-TO-AIR CODE

II	Require Medical Supplies
–	Require Doctor
F	Require Food and Water
III	Require Clothing
L	Require Fuel and Oil
O	Require Map and Compass
⌄⌄	Require Arms and Ammunition
W	Require Engineer
– –	Require Signal Lamp
⌐	Aircraft Badly Damaged

X	Unable to Proceed
I⟩	Will Attempt Take-off
→	We Proceed This Direction
K	Show Direction to Proceed
✳	Don't Land Here
←	Land Here, Pointing Direction
Y	Yes, Affirmative
N	No, Negative
⌐L	Not Understood
LL	All Well

BODY SIGNALS

Require Doctor   Use Drop Message   Require Mechanical Help or Parts   Our Receiver Operating   Can Proceed, or Wait

Pick Us Up Aircraft Abandoned   Land Here, Pointing Direction   Don't Land Here   Yes, Affirmative   No, Negative   All Well

(This is a true story about life in the early days quoted in a book about Salluit called *Eskimos Without Igloos.*)

"There were many hard times when food was scarce. Like the winter when the seals disappeared. Our supplies had been almost used up and we decided to go inland to hunt for Caribou ... At last we got up over onto land. We burned the sleds to cook the dogs on as our supplies were now all gone. My brother and his wife had a little Caribou at their house and he brought us a few bits.

"My brother left his wife to come with us to hunt for food. My oldest sister and her husband brought us a few bits of food and then left us to go look for food. Since we had no sled we used a polar bear skin as a sled and dragged it along over the snow. Two more days and nights went by and all we had to eat was one ptarmigan ... People were abandoning their own children. Mother was cutting up her own clothes to eat and the skin we were dragging was not large enough for a qaa (bedding sheet) because we were always eating it. In the end there was nothing left except the bare flat ground!

"Then, after two sleeps, we saw four Caribou. My brother, who was a great hunter, would never miss the sighting of a Caribou, but he was so weak from hunger he did not even notice them. We made motions like a Caribou in order to get close enough to shoot our arrows. One was wounded and the others ran away. If we had not been so weak we would have got at least three of them. In the morning we were able to get two more. Although we had plenty of meat for a short time, this soon ran out and we were hungry again. As we moved along, we finally came to Salluit when the snows were beginning to melt and we were not starved any more. We stayed in Salluit and that is where I grew up.

Make a chart to compare the modern way of Caribou hunting with the old way that Grandpa told about. Use sketches to show the different pieces of equipment used.

Modern Method	Old Method

1. In what way is each piece of modern equipment more efficient than its old counterpart?

2. How do the new methods and equipment affect
a) the number of animals a man can hunt?
b) the number of animals left after a few years of hunting?

Things To Do

1. Divide your class into small groups. Let each group take a small section of Grandpa's story, talk about it and then act out the story as a play. You may wish to add extra details that Grandpa omitted.
2. Make a mural showing the events of the story.
3. Put your play on for another class to see.

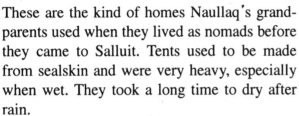

These are the kind of homes Naullaq's grandparents used when they lived as nomads before they came to Salluit. Tents used to be made from sealskin and were very heavy, especially when wet. They took a long time to dry after rain.

1. About how big are the tents and the snowhouse? How are the size of these homes and the materials used to build them suited to the old way of life of the Inuit and to hunting expeditions?

2. From the list below, choose the items the Inuit would need when they lived as nomads. Explain your choices.
   stove
   knives
   refrigerator
   animal hides
   sleeping bags
   soapstone
   air conditioner
   furniture
   snowshoes
   warm clothing

thermal underwear
sunglasses
dishes, glassware
bathing suit
motor boat
ropes
toboggan
sled
furnace
canned goods
oil lamp

Friendliness, sharing and co-operation are important in Inuit society. "Within the first week," writes a visitor to Salluit, "at least 120 people came to visit and share my food. Very soon my supply of food ran low and the tables were turned; for most of the summer I spent my time visiting Inuit households and sharing in their food and drinks and conversation. They never excluded me from sharing at any time of day or night."

The Annual Cycle

The traditional life of the Inuit was divided into two very different parts according to the time of year—summer and winter. Not all Inuit lived exactly alike, but here is a typical example of what the yearly cycle would have been like for many:

During the summer, when the ice and snow disappeared and the plants and animals returned, the Inuit would spread out across the land in small bands or family groups, hunting caribou, fishing in the lakes and streams, gathering berries and other plants, enjoying the variety of food that was available during the short arctic warm season. As winter approached and days grew shorter, the people would move back toward the coast, gathering into larger groups. Some groups carried out large scale, organized hunts in order to lay in a last supply of walrus, whale, or caribou meat before the ice and darkness of winter closed in.

During the depths of winter, the people huddled together in villages that contained as many as a dozen families. These villages were built on or near the sea ice so that the men could go out and hunt seals, which were the staple food for the people until the sun and warmth of spring returned and the cycle began again.

Spearing fish in a summer stream. What have the hunters done to make the work easier?

Draw up a chart like the one below and do research to see if you can fill in details of how the Inuit lived in the old days. Topics might be divided among different members of the class. Could you draw a panorama to show the life of the Inuit in summer and in winter?

Yearly Cycle Chart	Summer	Winter
Where the people lived		
What they lived in		
Size of the group		
How they travelled		
How they hunted		
What they wore		

TRADITIONAL FOODS OF THE INUIT

Type of Food	Seasonal Availability	Method of Getting Food	Location of Food
Caribou	Main hunting season—summer	Hunting (men)	Migrating herds
Seal	Year round	Hunting (men)	Coastal waters
Arctic Hare	Winter	Hunting (men)	Arctic region
Arctic Char	Spring and Summer	Fishing (men)	Coastal waters
Mussels	Spring and Summer	Gathered at low tide by women	Coastal waters
Clams	Spring and Summer	Gathered at low tide by women	Coastal waters
Lake Trout	Spring and Summer	Fishing (men)	Inland lakes and rivers
Sea Sculpins	Spring and Summer	Gathered along shore by women	Found along the shoreline
Seaweed	Summer	Gathered by women	Along shoreline
Small bushes containing berries	Summer	Gathered by women	Scattered growth in Arctic regions

1. How long ago did the Inuit as a people obtain all their food by the above methods?

2. What percentage of Inuit obtain all their food this way now?

3. What percentage of Inuit obtain some of their food this way now?

4. Add this information to your yearly-cycle chart. What does it suggest about the traditional Inuit way of life?

5. Make a list of foods the Inuit eat today and compare it with their traditional diet under the following headings: availability, variety, source, cost, how obtained.

Did You Know?

Inuit communities were usually very small in the old days. During the summer, a typical hunting group might be made up of only one or two families. Even when several groups came together during the winter the village was not large—usually from 15 to 60 people.

Hunting Seals

Seals were the mainstay of the traditional diet for almost all Inuit. Ringed seals are the most abundant species, while bearded seals are the largest. A bearded seal might weigh over 400 kilograms and, if it is cut properly, one skin can provide as much as 100 metres of strong line for rope, dog harnesses, harpoon line or many other uses.

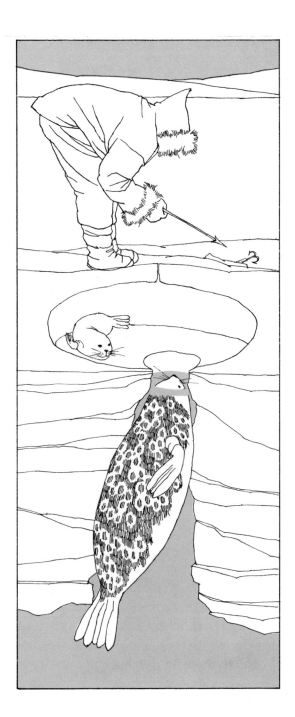

I. Examine the gaff lying on the ice beside Kanguq. What do you think this is for?

2. How has Kanguq protected himself from the biting cold?

3. In what ways would a husky dog be more useful than a snowmobile on a seal hunt?

4. Sometimes a hunter will stand for four or five hours without moving, waiting for a seal to come up for air. What does this suggest about the Inuit?

Did You Know?

The Inuit word for year, "ukiak," is the same as the Inuit word for winter. In late September the fresh lakes freeze over. By November the sea itself begins to freeze and form a big mass of ice offshore called the tuvak. Snow falls from November to April.

Approximately seven or eight kilometres was the farthest that it was practical for a hunter to walk in search of seals. During the winter months the Inuit might move their villages several times, whenever the seals in a particular area had been hunted out. The new village would be located approximately 15 kilometres from the old one. Can you explain?

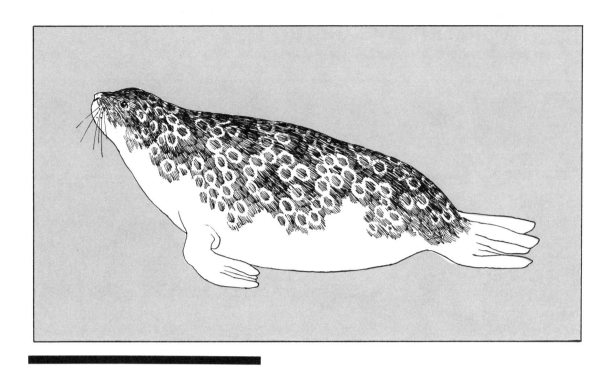

Head, eyes, front limbs, middle backbone meat and heart ....Women

Upper and lower backbone and meat...Men

Rib and chest meat ....Hunter who killed it

Lower back meat ....Men in the hunting party

Tail and hind flippers ....Cooked into a broth and eaten by all

Skin goes to the successful hunter and his party ....Scraps are fed to the dogs.

1. After examining the pictures and chart, what can you tell us about cooperation among the hunters?

2. How is the hunter who killed the seal rewarded?

3. What evidence is there to indicate that the Inuit are not selfish?

4. What different uses would the Inuit make of the seal?

Many of the animals above are called *Nigiksak* or "that which is able or about to be food."

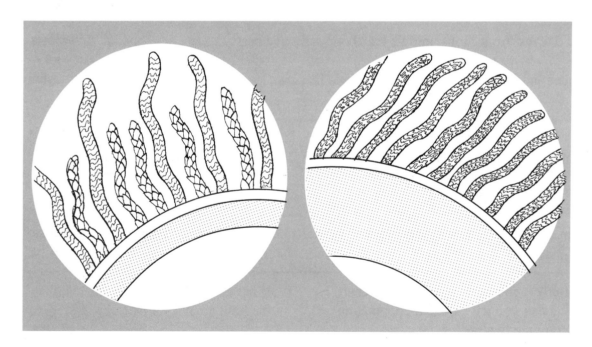

Notice the short hair close to the skin. How would this protect the bear?

The seal fur has an oily film on it. What advantage is this?

1. What features of these animals protect them
   a) from the harsh Arctic climate?
   b) from the hunters?

2 Which animal skins would be most useful? Why?

Did You Know?

The coastal area near Salluit can supply only about 400 seals per year without seriously endangering the seal population. This number would support just four hunters!

In 1966, 20 Husky dogs were shot because they ·were of little use and were expensive to keep. The snowmobile is rapidly taking the place of the Husky in the Arctic.

Lemmings are often called suicide animals because every few years great numbers of them plunge off cliffs into the sea. What really happens is that the lemmings sense there are too many of their species for the land in the region to support, so they swim until they come to land where there is more room. Many lemmings do, however, drown on these migrations.

"Lemmings live on sun-nourished vegetation and in turn themselves become food for the Arctic fox and the snowy owl to complete a simple food chain. They multiply fast, often having several litters a year from four to six kits. The sight of a lemming seems to stimulate the sex glands of the snowy owl and increases the number of owl eggs produced. Thus in times when the lemmings are abundant, the snowy owl and the fox both produce large litters."

The Arctic Coast by Douglas Wilkinson, National Science of Canada Ltd., 1970.

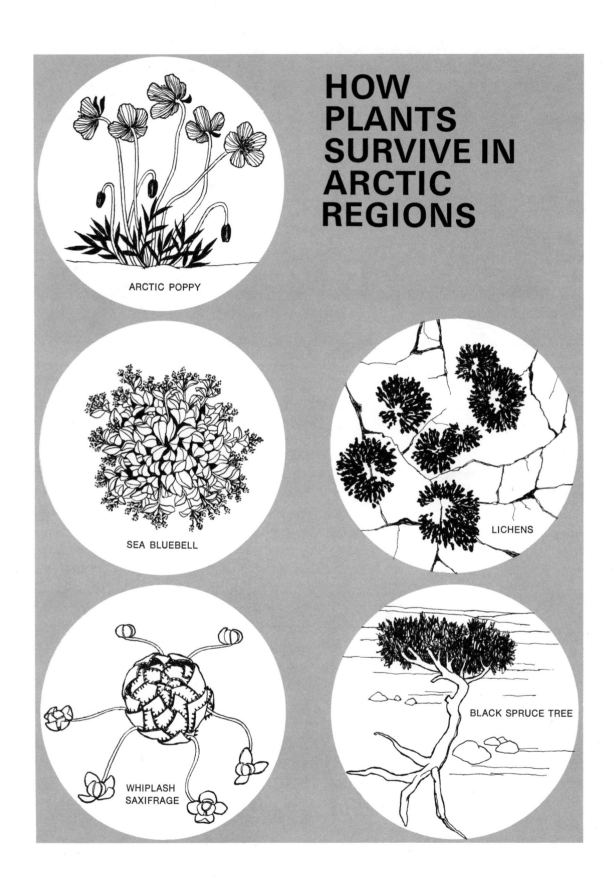

HOW PLANTS SURVIVE IN ARCTIC REGIONS

ARCTIC POPPY

SEA BLUEBELL

LICHENS

WHIPLASH SAXIFRAGE

BLACK SPRUCE TREE

How Plants Survive in Arctic Regions

1. Why is it difficult for plants to exist in Arctic regions?

2. How does the Arctic poppy insulate itself against the cold?

3. On a cold day, are you warmer standing by yourself or in a group?

4. How does the cluster of leaves and flowers help to insulate the sea bluebell from the cold?

5. How does the moss, on which the whiplash saxifrage grows, protect the plant?

6. How does the size of the lichen protect it from the cold?

7. How has the Arctic climate altered the normal growth of the black spruce tree?

Things To Do

1. How do the Arctic plants adjust to
a) the long periods of sunlight in summer?
b) weather so cold that there may be frost on any given day of the year?

2. Compare this to the burst of plant life after a sudden rainfall on a hot desert.

3. Find out what "physiological" drought is. Explain how these Arctic plants have to meet this problem.

Did You Know?

The Inuit often used the fibres of the Arctic cotton plant as a wick for their soapstone lamp, the koolik.

The Koolik

The koolik is an invention that allowed the Inuit to have light, heat and cooked food throughout the winter in a region where there was no wood.

1. Look at the illustrations and describe how the koolik works.

2. How have the Inuit combined three different elements "animal, vegetable and mineral" to produce the koolik?

3. The koolik is an example of a technology that is perfectly adapted to the natural environment in which it was used. What does this statement mean? Do you agree or disagree?

4. What disadvantages might there be in using the koolik?

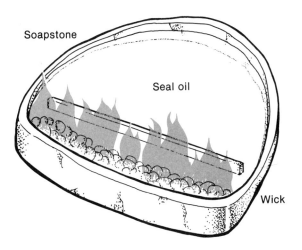

Soapstone

Seal oil

Wick

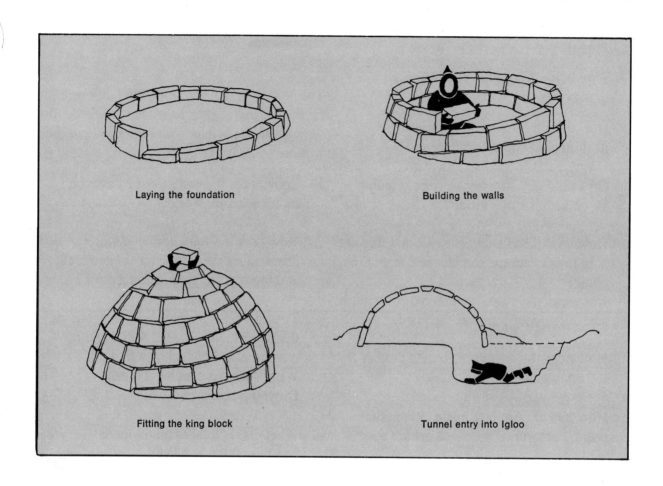

Laying the foundation

Building the walls

Fitting the king block

Tunnel entry into Igloo

Block of clear ice in roof gave light.

Raised sleeping platform was called an illiq.

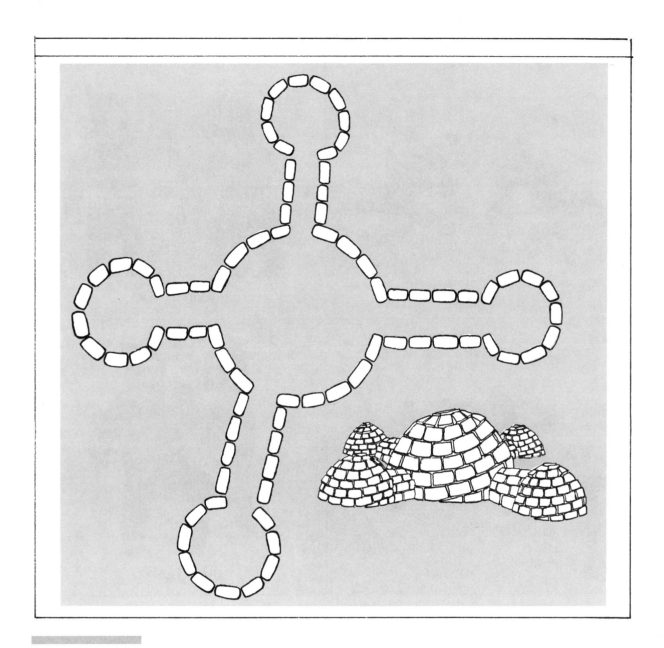

Did You Know?

"Igloo" is a word meaning house in general in Inuktitut. The snowhouse, which is what we usually think of as an igloo, might be anything from a small one-person overnight shelter built by a hunter on the trail, to a large, carefully-built structure that might be the home of an entire family for several months.

In some winter villages, an extra-large igloo (like the one shown above) might be built as a community meeting place. During the long winter nights the people would gather in the community igloo for festivals, storytelling, singing, dances and games.

AJARAQ

NULLATTARTUQ

TUNUMMIJUK

ARSAARARTUQ

Traditional Inuit Games

1. What are the people doing in each of these games or activities?

2. Are any of them similar to games that you play?

3. Which of these activities involve strength? Which need agility and co-ordination?

Which games show competition? Which games need co-operation? How would each of these things be important to the Inuit in their struggle to survive? How do their games help teach useful skills?

4. Try playing some of these Inuit games.

QUMUAQATAIJUT

AJJAGATUK

AJUTATUT

KILAUJATUT

KALIVITATUT

ILUKITATUK

WHERE THE INUIT LIVE

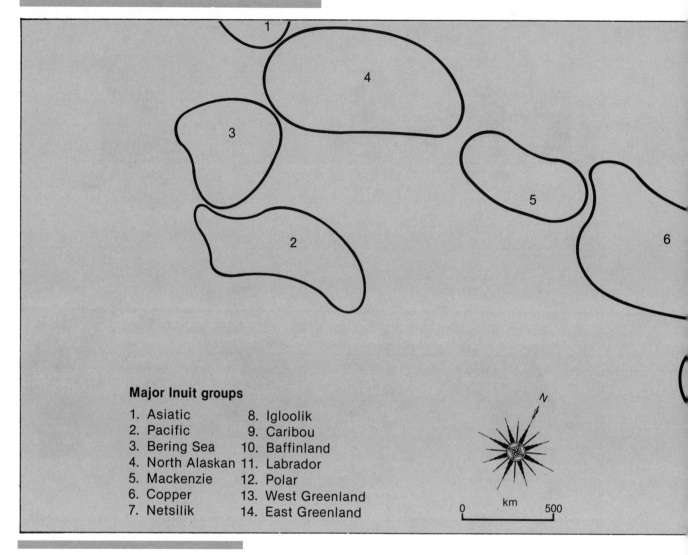

Major Inuit groups

1. Asiatic
2. Pacific
3. Bering Sea
4. North Alaskan
5. Mackenzie
6. Copper
7. Netsilik
8. Igloolik
9. Caribou
10. Baffinland
11. Labrador
12. Polar
13. West Greenland
14. East Greenland

0   km   500

Where the Inuit Lived in the Past

Although they were spread out over thousands of kilometres of the harsh Arctic, the original Inuit all spoke the same language and shared the same basic culture. There were, however, minor differences from place to place.

The Inuit were usually divided into fourteen major groups. Each group spoke a slightly different dialect of Inuktitut. Each group had different ways of hunting. The Polar, Labrador, and Mackenzie people got most of their food from the sea, and spent only a small part of the year hunting caribou. The Caribou people usu-ally hunted the caribou all year round. They only occasionally visited the ocean to hunt seals and whales. Within each major group there were many smaller local groupings. For example, the people who lived in the region around Salluit called themselves the Takamiut. (The ending *miut* means "people who live in." *Takak* means "darkness" or "shadow.") The Takamiut were not a tribe. There was no central organization, no chief or overall leader. The Takamiut were made up of many small, independent hunting bands who lived in the area along the south side of Hudson Strait.

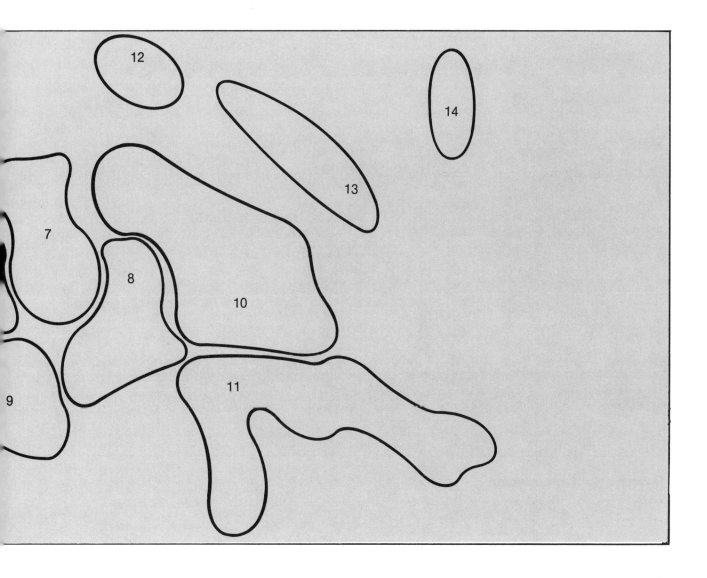

1. Where did most of the Inuit live in relation to the sea coast? What does this suggest about their way of life?

2. Where did most of the Inuit live in relation to the tree line? What does this suggest about their way of life?

3. The total Inuit population was probably never more than 100 000. According to the map above, about how big an area did the Inuit occupy? About how many people were there per square kilometre?

4. What is a dialect? How is it different from a language? How do dialects start?
    Are there any dialects in English or French?

Did You Know?

All told, there are still about 100 000 Inuit alive today. They live in the eastern tip of Siberia, Alaska, Canada, and Greenland. About 23 000 live in Canada.

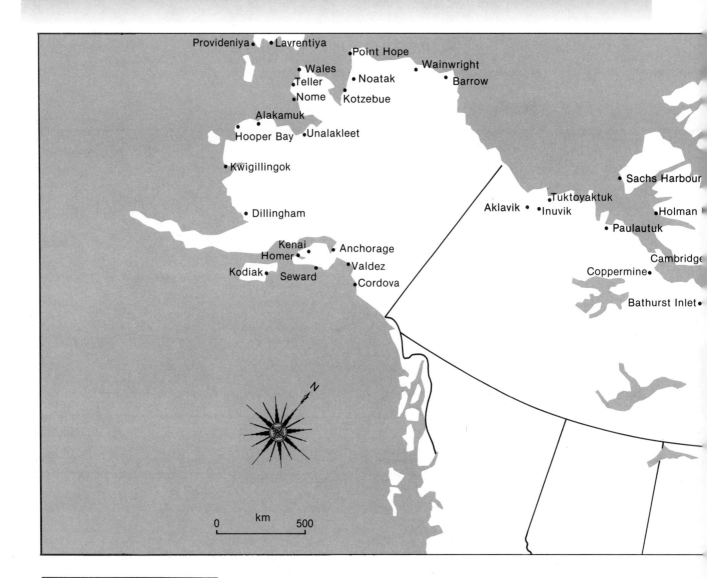

Provideniya • • Lavrentiya
•Point Hope
• Wales   • Wainwright
•Teller   • Noatak   • Barrow
•Nome   Kotzebue
Alakamuk
•   •Unalakleet
Hooper Bay
• Kwigillingok
                                    • Sachs Harbour
                              .Tuktoyaktuk
                    Aklavik • •Inuvik   •Holman
• Dillingham   • Paulautuk
Kenai
Homer• • Anchorage   Cambridge
Kodiak•   •Valdez   Coppermine•
Seward   •Cordova
                                    Bathurst Inlet •

km
0   500

Where the Inuit Live Now

Look at the map to find out where most of the Inuit live now.

What does this map suggest about the way of life of the Inuit in the modern world?

The Inuit of the northern Quebec area now live in fifteen communities along the shores of Ungava Bay, Hudson Strait and Hudson Bay.

1. According to the figures, what is the total Inuit population in Northern Quebec?

2. Which place has the largest Inuit population?

3. Arrange the communities according to size. Where are the largest concentrations of Inuit?

4. How many non-Inuit are there? Who might they be and where might they come from?

5. What do the names of the communities suggest about the history of this area?

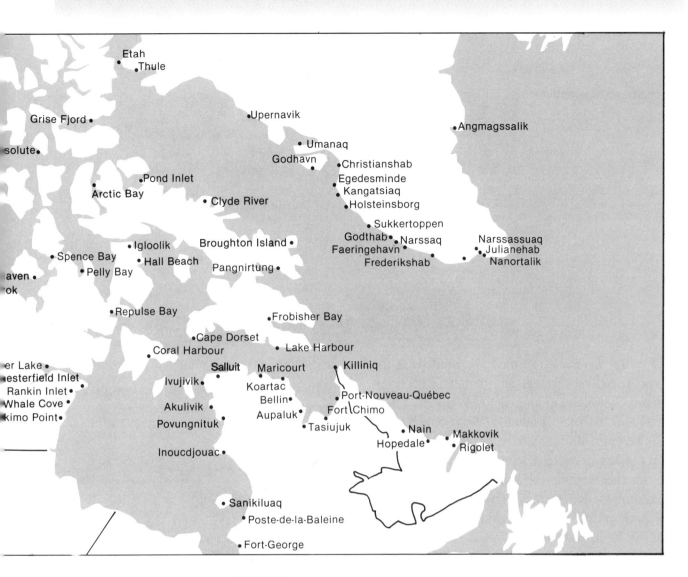

	Inuit	Total
Population of Northern Quebec		
Akulivik	140	140
Aupaluk	20	20
Bellin (Payne)	274	285
Fort-Chimo (Kuujjuak)	688	915
Fort-George	53	1833
Inoucdjouac (Port Harrison)	586	604
Ivujivik	168	173
Koartac	126	132
Maricourt (Wakeham)	244	256
Port-Nouveau-Québec (Kangiqsualujjuak)	271	282
Poste-de-la-Baleine (Great Whale River) (Kuujjuaraapik)	558	1101
Povungnituk	700	752
Salluit (Saglouc Sugluk)	501	526
Tasiujaq (Baie-aux-Feuilles)	95	98
Killiniq (Port Burwell)	77	82

The first Europeans to meet the Inuit were the Norse traders, farmers and hunters who colonized Greenland as long ago as 986 A.D. These early colonizers gradually died out by the 1300s and 1400s, and for many years there was no contact between Europeans and Inuit at all.

In the 1500s, following the voyages of Columbus and Cabot, explorers, traders and fishermen from Europe again came to the land of the Inuit. However, there was very little contact between the Inuit and the Europeans (or Qallunak, as the Inuit called them).

The first European to reach the region where the Takamiut lived, for example, was probably Henry Hudson. Although his ships explored Hudson Strait and Hudson Bay in 1610, he and his crew did not stop in the Salluit area. In the years that followed, many other ships also passed through the region on their way to and from the trading posts on Hudson Bay, but there continued to be only limited contact.

1. What products were the early Europeans looking for when they came to the Americas? Are these things found in the High Arctic where the Inuit live?

2. What other reasons can you think of why there was little contact between Europeans and Inuit for many years?

3. Why do you think the Inuit did not travel south to trade at the early Hudson's Bay Company posts on James Bay and Hudson Bay?

Did You Know?

During the nineteenth century many whaling ships began to visit the Arctic. These ships would sometimes meet groups of Inuit and trade with them. However, no permanent trading post was established in the region until 1866. In that year the Hudson's Bay Company opened a permanent trading post at Fort Chimo on Ungava Bay. For the first time, the Takamiut had a regular source of European trade goods within reach of their territory. Inuit from as far away as the Salluit area went there to trade. The journey to and from the trading post might take half a year or even longer. A few strong and experienced men would be chosen to make the trip and trade on behalf of everyone in the group. The main trade item was the fur of the Arctic fox, though mink and seal skins were also traded.

Here are some dates from history. What do they suggest about the growth of Salluit as a settled community?

B.C.

3000:   Humans first learn to live in the Arctic regions

500:    First humans reach Salluit area

A.D.

1497:   Sebastian Cabot sails to Newfoundland and the Grand Banks

1610:   Henry Hudson explores Hudson Bay

1670:   Hudson's Bay Company established

1866:   Hudson's Bay post built at Fort Chimo

1890:   Anglican missionaries begin visits along the coast

1902:   Rev. Stewart of the Anglican Church visits Salluit area

1904:   A. P. Low, a government geologist, visits Salluit area

1916:   Independent trader sets up post at Salluit

1927:   Hudson's Bay Company post established at Salluit

1927:   First Inuit family starts using Salluit as a permanent base

1930:   More families begin using Salluit as a permanent base

1940:   More families move to Salluit area

1947:   Permanent Catholic mission built

1949:   First Salluit carvings sold through Hudson's Bay store

1955:   Permanent Anglican missionary comes to Salluit

1957:   First wooden houses supplied by the government

1957:   Federal school built

1960:   Nursing station built

1963:   First snowmobile bought by Inuit

1967:   Salluit Co-op established

1970:   Inuit land claims discussed

1975:   James Bay and Northern Quebec Agreement signed

1. How far is it from Salluit to Fort Chimo? How long would it take to get there if you were travelling
   a) by airplane at 200 km/h?
   b) by snowmobile at 30 km/h?
   c) by dog team at 5 km/h?
   d) on foot at 3 km/h?

2. What goods would the Hudson's Bay Company trader ask for? Why would these probably be different from the goods traded to sailors or explorers on ships?

3. What goods would the Inuit ask for at the Hudson's Bay Company post? Would these be different from the goods traded from the sailors? Why or why not?

Did You Know?

As recently as the first years of the twentieth century there were some groups of Inuit who had never seen a white man.

The Anglican Church in Salluit

Missionaries

By the early 1900s, European missionaries were beginning to visit the North to bring their religion to the Inuit. The first missionaries in the Salluit area came from the Anglican Church. They travelled from place to place by sled and converted the people to Christianity. The Anglicans did not build a permanent mission, but instead visited each settlement regularly. They appointed Inuit in each area to represent the church while the missionaries were away. The missionaries' influence was greater than the religion they brought. They wanted the Inuit to be able to read the Bible, but the Inuit did not have a written language. Inuktitut was only spoken. The Anglican missionaries developed a syllabic writing which came to be used by the Inuit in the eastern Arctic.

1. Before the coming of the missionaries, the Inuit believed that the world was inhabited by many spirits. See if you can find out about the former beliefs of the Inuit.

2. Can you find any illustrations of Inuit prints that show what the people believed the spirits looked like?

3. Shamans were people who claimed to be able to communicate with the spirits. They were important and powerful people because they could bring bad luck to someone they did not like. See if you can find out about shamans and what they did.

Serious illness or injury means an airplane trip to a hospital down South.

When white people first went to the North, they unwittingly carried diseases to a healthy community. Inuit had never developed a resistance to lung diseases and many died from tuberculosis (TB). In 1950, when the Canadian government realized what was happening, they sent a hospital ship so that all the all Inuit could have a health check. Inuit with TB were sent to sanitoriums to recover. Gradually the problem was overcome. Since 1960 there has been a nursing station in Salluit with a consulting room and a two-bed emergency room. Two nurses look after the health care of the people. Children in the schools in Salluit are given regular checkups by the nurses. The children are served hot lunches and the nurses help parents learn about caring for the children when they are sick. Serious maternity and surgical patients must be flown to Montreal for treatment. Unfortunately, there is no doctor living in Salluit.

1. What kind of problems might the Inuit face when they go to Montreal for surgery or hospital care?

2. Why has tooth care become a problem in the Arctic?

Did You Know?

In the old days, the Inuit believed that disease or misfortune was caused by the spirits. If someone fell sick, the shaman was called in to find out why the spirits were angry and to ask them to let the person get well.

EDUCATION IN SALLUIT

The Federal School in Salluit

When Naullaq's father was a young boy, he didn't go to school. An Anglican missionary taught him the basics of reading and writing, but everything else he learned from his father and the other men. Now there are five schools in Salluit and Naullaq attends regularly. Only when there is a special event—like the grand caribou hunt described earlier, for example—is Naullaq allowed to not attend.

The first school was built in Salluit in 1957. In the beginning the children only went to school if they happened to be in the area. If there was an ordinary hunting trip, the children would go off with their families, even if school was in session. Then, early in the 1960s, the government began to insist that Inuit children attend school fulltime. The parents did not want to be separated from their children, so they went hunting less and less. Attendance at school was one of the main reasons why Salluit became a fully permanent settlement.

In the early days, the school was run by the federal government. All the teachers were Qallunak from the south. English was used. Many students had difficulty speaking languages other than Inuktitut and found school discouraging as a result. Now Inuktitut is used much more and English and French are taught as subjects.

Since 1977, the Inuit have run the schools themselves through the Kativik School Board. The Kativik School Board was formed as a result of the Northern Quebec Agreement and is responsible for all education in northern Quebec. One person is elected to the board from each community. Together these people decide how the schools will be run. The school system in Salluit now has a certified teacher who is Inuit, with an Inuit assistant. As education among the Inuit increases, more and more of the Inuit will themselves become available to teach.

When Naullaq reaches high school age, he could go to the all-Inuit high school in Montreal, which was opened by the Kativik School Board in 1978. Courses are offered in English, French and Inuktitut that enable Inuit youths to learn trades needed in the north.

Naullaq's parents want Naullaq to be well educated so that he can get a good job when he grows up. But they also want him to know and remember the old Inuit ways. Thus, Naullaq is also being taught important things by his father and grandfather, such as hunting, fishing, canoeing and other skills, things that he doesn't learn at school.

Differing Opinions

1. Make up a list of subjects that Naullaq might study in school. Will you include any special subjects that you don't study in your school? Why or why not? Will you leave out any of the subjects that you study? Why or why not?

2. Should Naullaq study these courses in Inuktitut, English or French? Give reasons for your answer.

3. Should Naullaq study some subjects in Inuktitut and some in English or French? If so, which? Give reasons for your answer.

4. How would you feel if you had to do your school work in Inuktitut?

There are actually many different opinions among Inuit parents, and between parents and the Kativik School Board, about how Inuit children might best be educated.

The Inuit see their lives in a different way than do people to the south. Because of this, the idea of formal education is sometimes confusing to the Inuit. Their previous experience of learning goes back to the time when people lived close to the land and to each other. In the old days, children learned what they needed to know from their parents and other family members. Now, when Canadian culture is offered to them, they feel torn between the old ways and the new.

One Inuit parent says, "Inuit want their kids to understand the Qallunak society. But it's working backwards, because the Qallunak are trying to make Qallunak out of us."

The life of the Inuit has changed with incredible speed in a very short time. In one generation, the people have gone from a nomadic life of tents, snowhouses and dog teams to a world of snowmobiles, permanent wooden homes, schools, airplanes and TV satellite dishes.

The Inuit have adapted to these changes with panache and imagination, but many people in Salluit and other communities across the Canadian Arctic are asking themselves serious questions about the future. Should the Inuit leave the land behind and get jobs in the towns? Will there be enough jobs for all? If so, where will they learn the skills that are needed for these jobs? Should they give up Inuktitut and learn English or French? Should the Inuit give up their old ways completely and try to become like Canadians?

Sometimes modern technology proves unreliable. For instance, if a snowmobile breaks down far away from a settlement, it is important to know hunting and igloo-building skills. The north is still the north.

Understanding how our forefathers lived is invaluable. In the old days, the young people learned from their parents, and were often exposed to the hardships and elements. When they saw firsthand how their elders went about their struggle for survival, they learned to respect nature, and, most of all, their parents. When a person knew how to live off the land without outside help, there was a greater sense of security and self confidence.

One Opinion

Here is one opinion, written by an Inuk:

In the days when dog teams and igloos were an everyday necessity, the only thing that kept the Inuit alive was their ability to hunt. Today is the time of the snowmobile and the frame house, and some people, especially the youth, ask, "Why bother about old traditions when I can earn a living doing a regular job?"

Today, most Inuit children go to modern schools with many conveniences where they are instructed by a teacher in a classroom. Although this form of instruction prepares them so they can live without hunting, they are still in the north.

1. Do you agree or disagree with these thoughts? Give your reasons.

2. What traditional skills do you think an Inuit child would need in order to live in the north today?

3. What non-traditional skills might Inuit children learn in school that could help them in the north?

The Inuit and the Land

By the time European explorers and traders first visited the north, the Inuit had already been living there for hundreds of years, close to the land and in harmony with it. Nature provided what they needed in order to survive. It was a fundamental part of their life. The Inuit have long believed that they hold special rights to the land where they and their ancestors have lived for so long. Until recently they had no idea that anyone else might have claims to their land.

Whose Land is it?

In 1610, the land where Salluit is located was formally claimed for England by the explorer Henry Hudson, and, in 1670, was given over to the Hudson's Bay Company by the King of England. In 1870 the area was officially made a part of Canada, and, in 1912, was placed within Quebec's borders.

Some Things to Think About

1. Does anyone in your family own a piece of land? If so, how did they first acquire it?

2. How can you prove that a piece of land belongs to you?

3. What happens if two people both claim that they own the same piece of land?

4. Suppose you find some land with nobody living on it. Can you live on the land and say that it is yours?

5. Suppose you don't live on the land all the time, but use it only part of the time. Does the land still belong to you? How could you prove it?

6. What do these questions have to do with Salluit?

THE NORTHERN QUEBEC AGREEMENT

Early in the 1970s, the government of Quebec decided to build a series of hydro-electric power stations on the rivers running into James Bay. The construction work and the giant dams across the rivers would have affected the lives of the Cree Indians living in the area. The Quebec government had never made an agreement with the Cree (or the Inuit) as to what lands belonged to them. With the coming of the James Bay project, Quebec decided to work out a settlement with all the native people of northern Quebec, including the Inuit. In 1975, after long negotiations, the James Bay and Northern Quebec Agreement was signed between the Cree, the Inuit and the governments of Quebec and Canada.

Highlights of the 1975 Northern Quebec Agreement

- The dark areas on the map to be designated Category 1 lands. These areas in and around each Inuit village to belong to the people of the village as a whole.
- The light areas to be designated Category 2 lands. In these areas only the Inuit to be allowed to hunt, fish, and trap.
- The Canadian and Quebec governments to pay $225 000 000 to the Native people (Crees and Inuit) over a 20-year period.
- All of Quebec north of 55° to be governed by the Kativik Regional Government, to be elected by the people who live there.
- Education in northern Quebec to be controlled by the Kativik School Board, also to be elected by the people who live in the north.

Allocation of land (in square kilometres)

Inuit Community	Category 1	Category 2
Fort-George	45.1	0
Poste-de-la-Baleine	585.8	8064.5
Inoucdjouac	557.8	8883.2
Povungnituk	626.6	8492.4
Akulivik	557.7	5190.9
Ivujivik	524.9	4576.3
Salluit	635.7	7013.0
Maricourt	606.7	5181.9
Koartac	477.7	4175.7
Bellin	629.5	4864.6
Aupaluk	629.8	4039.7
Tasiujaq	629.8	3840.3
Fort-Chimo	546.1	8880.4
Port-Nouveau-QuÇbec	539.6	5490.1
Killiniq	290.5	3903.7
Total	**7873.3**	**81596.7**

1. How much Category 1 land is there at Salluit? How much is this for each Inuk in the village?
2. How much Category 2 land is allotted for Inuit hunting, fishing and trapping around Salluit? How much is this for each Inuk?
3. The map does not show any lands set aside for the villages of Ivujivik and Povungnituk. Can you explain why?

While most of the Inuit have accepted the Northern Quebec Agreement, the people of Povungnituk, Ivujivik and some of the people of Salluit are opposed to it. They refuse to accept the agreement's terms and have formed an organization called Inuit Tungavinga Nunamini to protest against them.

The Makivik Corporation

The money being paid to the Inuit under the Northern Quebec Agreement is not being given directly to the people. Instead, it is being given to a company that is investing it. The name of this company is the Makivik Corporation. The Makivik Corporation is located in Kuujjuak (formerly Fort Chimo), but it is run by a board of directors from all the Inuit communities.

One of the projects that has been started by the company is Air Inuit, an Inuit-operated airline that made its first scheduled flight in May, 1978. This airline is a regional carrier for Ungava Bay and connects all Inuit communities from George River in the east to Wakeham Bay in the west.

The Makivik Corporation has set up many projects that will provide jobs, training and development for the Inuit, and is planning more.

1. What happens when you spend money? Is spending money easy to do?

2. What does it mean to invest money? Has anyone in your family ever invested money? How did they do it? Is investing easy to do?

3. What is the difference between spending money and investing money? Which is better? Explain your answer.

4. What have these questions got to do with the people of Salluit?

The Nunavut Plan

In the fall of 1979, the Inuit of the Northwest Territories presented to the Canadian government a document about a political plan for their part of the north. Inuit Tapirisat of Canada represents most of the Inuit in the Northwest Territories. This group is requesting that a 2.5 million square kilometre area north of the tree line and east of the Mackenzie Valley be set aside as a new territory for the people who live there. The majority of the people in this new territory would be Inuit. The name of the new territory would be *Nunavut*, the Inuit word for "Our Land."

1. How is the idea of Nunavut different from the Northern Quebec Agreement? Which do you think will give the Inuit more control over their own lives?

2. Find out more about the proposal for Nunavut. For information write to: Inuit Tapirisat of Canada, 176 Gloucester Street, Ottawa, ON K2P OA6.

INUKTITUT: THE INUIT LANGUAGE

As well as being concerned about their lands, many Inuit are worried about keeping their language alive. Language is a very important part of a culture. The Inuit are afraid that if they learn English or French and use these languages to get jobs, they will lose their identity as Inuit. When schools were first built in Salluit, the children had to use English in class. Now that education is controlled by the Inuit themselves through the Kativik School Board, more of the lessons are taught in Inuktitut, especially in lower grades.

Did You Know?

In the eastern Arctic, Inuktitut is written with special characters called syllabics. Syllabics were first invented by a Methodist missionary working with Cree Indians. In the 1930s, Anglican missionaries adapted the Cree syllabics for use with Inuktitut. Many Inuit learned to read and write using syllabics.

ᑕᒪᖅᐊᑕᐅᖅ ᓴᒍᐊᖏᓐ ᐅᑎᒥᕐᓲ ᐊᔪ-
ᐊᕟᖅ ᐅᑎ ᐁ ᑕᒪᑯᓂ ᐱᕝᐅᕐᐊᖅᑯ
ᐅᕐᐳᒍᐦ   ᔪᕐ ᐊᑐᓂ ᑯᐱᐊᑎᖅᑎ
ᕈᐦᒪᑦ   ᖅᑎᕐᓱᑎᖅ ᓗ ᐊᒪᓗ ᐊᑯᓂ
ᐱᕐᖻᐳᔪᐊᖅ ᕠᕀᕀ.

1. What do you think syllabics means? What does this suggest about Inuktitut? Would it be possible to use syllabic characters to write English words?

2. The symbols that we use to write words are collectively called the alphabet. What is an alphabet? How does it differ from a collection of syllabics?

3. Do you think the Inuit will be able to get good jobs if they speak only Inuktitut?

4. What do you think will happen to the Inuit culture if the children learn only English or French in school?

Did you Know?

In 1980, a small Inuit-operated TV network started broadcasting between five communities in the Northwest Territories. Now many Inuit communities have television.

When the government first offered to build television transmitters in northern Quebec, the people said they did not want them.

They said: "If it was just a hockey game we could watch it, but television also presents films of violence, and that will make our children violent. If that is your television, we do not want it."

A large TV studio has been set up in Salluit. An organization called Taqramiut Nipingat is training people from many Inuit communities to use the equipment and produce TV programs. Because of this, the songs, stories and traditions of the Inuit are now being preserved.

Change is coming to the North with incredible speed. The people of Salluit and other Inuit communities are learning new skills and new ideas that will let them be a part of the modern world.

On the other hand, many Inuit are sad to see the old ways disappearing. Many still love the wandering life of the hunter and trapper and feel the call of the land where their ancestors have lived for centuries.

In fact, some Inuit families are returning to the life they have always known. These families live in camps of two to five families. They want to live the traditional Inuit way, so they are teaching their children to gather food and to hunt, and are helping them learn what they must know to be Inuit. Years ago there were at least 700 camps. By the end of the 1960s only a dozen were left. Now there are again about 1000 people living in fifty camps. The government of the Northwest Territories is helping the families who wish to go back to the old ways. The call of the land is strong, and that is why these people have returned to the kind of life they love.

No one can say which way is better - the old or the new. Perhaps young Inuit children like Naullaq and Paani will be able to combine the best of both ways. Perhaps Naullaq and Paani will be able to take the best things from the world of the Qallunak and combine them with the culture and heritage of the Inuit.